SIMPLE GUIDE TO AIR FRYER

A Superlative Cookbook Guide To Understanding The Concepts Of Air Fryer Recipes For Everyday

Hollie McCarthy RDN

deemed liable for any hardship or damages that may befall them after undertaking information described herein.

Additionally, the information in the following pages is intended only for informational purposes and should thus be thought of as universal. As befitting its nature, it is presented without assurance regarding its prolonged validity or interim quality. Trademarks that are mentioned are done without written consent and can in no way be considered an endorsement from the trademark holder.

Table of Content

Introduction

Welcome to the air fryer guide!

The air fryer is one of the most impressive and useful inventions of the decade. With this machine, you can reduce the amount of grease you consume from traditional dishes and snacks such as chicken nuggets and French fries. Goes without saying that cooking time is considerably reduced!

It is a multi-cooker that performs more than functions. The air fryer enables you to cook a wide variety of dishes including meat, fish, eggs, grain, poultry, beans, cakes, yogurt and vegetables etc. What Serves: it exceptional is because you can use different cooking programs such as a steamer, rice cooker, sauté pan, and even a warming pot, thus saving more time, money, and space than buying any other kitchen appliances.

The Air fryer Serves: as a multi-use programmable appliance can help create easy, fast and flavorful recipes with the ability to apply different cooking settings all in one pot. It was developed by Canadian technology experts seeking to be the ultimate kitchen mate, from stir-frying, pressure cooking, slow cooking and yogurt and cake making. It was created to serve as a one-stop shop to allow home cooks prepare a tasty meal with the press of a button. You can cook almost everything in this fryer.

The air fryer uses an ingenious combination of both Directions, differing from the convection oven because heat circulates everywhere (vice rising to the top) through the fan, and not through the turbo because there is typically no heating element in the top of a fryer from where the heat comes out. They use electrical energy to create their heat; a lot of power!

Many people still have their doubts regarding the importance of this machine, and what a healthy alternative it can be. Despite its popularity, in some regions it has not yet reached the peak of its use. It is very likely that in a short time new brands will emerge in other regions and the air fryer will grow in popularity across the nation.

The use of this tool consists of cooking something without boiling the product in oil or fat. At most, the maximum oil needed by the air fryer is a tablespoon, which is used to prevent the food from sticking and forming an overdone crust.

What is an air fryer?

An air fryer works with "fast air technology." This means that there is a highspeed circulation of hot air that cocoons the food you cook.

During this process, the air fryer prepares the food evenly, all the while giving it a "fried" taste and texture without ever actually having to fry anything in grease.

While many people and regions near and far are familiar with this tool, the electric fryer is even crossing the waters. They are even found commonly in Europe and Australia!

The air fryer is similar in concept to a convection oven or a turbo grill, although the fryer still differs slightly from both appliances. Convection ovens and turbo broilers depend on different heating Directions and are often larger and bulkier appliances to use when cooking your food.

In this book, we will explore the variety of easy delicious dishes you can cook with your air fryer. We will explore a wide variety of dishes, from breakfast to dinner, soups to stews, desserts to appetizers, meat to beef, side dishes to vegetables and use a healthy ingredient in the process. The vast majority of the recipes can be prepared and served in less than 45 minutes. Each recipe is written with the exact cooking Directions and ingredients required to prepare dishes that will satisfy and nourish you. Once you try the delish dishes in this cookbook, you and your air fryer are sure to become inseparable too.

It's important to think outside the box when it comes to trying out recipes in your air fryer. From roasted vegetables to empanadas, to baked eggs and vegan brownies, there's an option for everyone when you use your air fryer.

This cookbook is for people who want to create tasty dishes without spending all day in the kitchen. Most of the recipes can be prepared in 15 minutes or less. And most of them can be on the table in under an hour. With today's busy lifestyles, I know this is important to most of you.

In keeping with the latest health trends and diets, the recipes also include complete nutrition information. As a plus, there are recipes for those on a Vegan Diet as well as Mediterranean diet.

Let's delve in!

Serves: 4

INGREDIENTS

- 3 eggs, beaten
- 2 tbsp unsalted butter ½ cup flour
- 2 tbsp sugar, powdered
- ½ cup milk
- 1½ cups fresh strawberries, sliced

DIRECTIONS

1. Preheat your Air Fryer to 330 degrees F. Add butter to a pan and melt over low heat. In a bowl, mix flour, milk, eggs, and vanilla until fully incorporated. Add the mixture to the pan with melted butter.

2. Place the pan in your air fryer's cooking basket and cook for 12-16 minutes until the pancake is fluffy and golden brown. Drizzle powdered sugar and toss sliced strawberries on top.

Per serving: Calories: 196; Carbs:19g; Fat: 9g; Protein: 16g

Grilled Apple and Brie Sandwich

Serve: 1

INGREDIENTS

- 2 bread slices
- ½ apple, thinly sliced
- 2 tsp butter
- 2 oz brie cheese, thinly sliced

DIRECTIONS

1. Spread butter on the outside of the bread slices. Arrange apple slices on the inside of one bread slice. Place brie slices on top of

the apple. Top with the other slice of bread. Cook for 5 minutes at 350 F.

2. Serve cut diagonally.

Per serving: Calories: 391; Carbs:27.8 g; Fat: 25.9 g; Protein: 18 g

Serve: 1

INGREDIENTS

- ⅓ cup shredded leftover turkey
- ⅓ cup sliced mushrooms
- 1 tbsp butter, divided
- 2 tomato slices
- ½ tsp red pepper flakes

- ¼ tsp salt
- ¼ tsp black pepper
- 1 hamburger bun

DIRECTIONS

1. Melt half of the butter and add the mushrooms. Cook for 4 minutes. Meanwhile, cut the bun in half and spread the remaining butter on the outside of the bun.

2. Place the turkey on one half of the bun. Arrange the mushroom slices on top of the turkey. Place the tomato slices on top of the mushrooms.

   Sprinkle with salt pepper and red pepper flakes. Top with the other bun half. Cook for 5 minutes at 350 F.

Per serving: Calories: 315; Carbs:25.6 g; Fat: 16.4 g; Protein: 18.4 g

Garlicky Chicken on Green Bed

Serve: 1

INGREDIENTS

- ½ cup baby spinach leaves
- ½ cup shredded romaine
- 3 large kale leaves, chopped
- 4 oz chicken breasts, cut into cubes
- 3 tbsp olive oil, divided
- 1 tsp balsamic vinegar
- 1 garlic clove, minced
- Salt and pepper, to taste

DIRECTIONS

1. Place the chicken, 1 tbsp. olive oil and garlic, in a bowl. Season with salt and pepper and toss to combine.

2. Put on a lined baking dish and cook for 14 minutes at 390F. Meanwhile, place the greens in a large bowl. Add the remaining clive oil and balsamic vinegar. Season with salt and pepper and toss to combine. Top with the chicken.

Per serving: Calories: 551; Carbs:10.7 g; Fat: 45 g; Protein: 28.7 g

Serve: 1

INGREDIENTS

- 3 eggs
- 3 tbsp cottage cheese
- 3 tbsp chopped kale
- ½ tbsp chopped basil
- ½ tbsp chopped parsley
- Salt and pepper, to taste
- 1 tsp olive oil

DIRECTIONS

1. Heat oil at 330 F. Beats the eggs with salt and pepper, in a bowl.

2. Stir in the rest of the ingredients. Pour the mixture into the air fryer and cook for 10 minutes, until slightly golden and set.

Per serving: Calories: 294; Carbs: 3.9 g; Fat: 19.5 g; Protein: 24.7 g

Picante Lamb Chops

Serves: 6

Ingredients

- 6 lamb chops, bone-in
- 1¼ apples, peeled and sliced
- 1¼ cup Picante sauce
- 3 tablespoons olive oil
- 3 tablespoons all-purpose flour
- 3 tablespoons brown sugar, packed

Directions

1. Dredge the lamb chops through a bowl of flour.

2. Mix the apple slices, Picante sauce, and brown sugar in a bowl.

3. Pour the oil into the Air Fryer and select 'sauté'.

4. Add the flour-covered chops to the oil and sear for 5 minutes.

5. Secure the lid and select the 'meat stew" function. Cook for 35 minutes at high pressure.

6. Once done 'Natural release' the steam for 10 minutes, then remove the lid. 7. Serve warm.

Nutrition Values (Per Serving): Calories: 449 | Carbohydrate: 16.3g | Protein: 20.1g | Fat: 33.3g

Serves: 3

Ingredients

- ½ pork tenderloin

- ½ tablespoon ground cumin

- 1 teaspoon salt

- ½ tablespoon chili powder

- ½ tablespoon garlic powder

- ½ tablespoon butter

- 4 cups water

- 3 calabacita squashes, seeds removed

Directions

1. Season the pork with half the cumin, garlic powder, salt, and chili powder.
2. Switch the Air Fryer to 'sauté' mode and add the butter to heat.
3. Place the seasoned pork in the pot and cook it for 4 minutes per side.
4. Pour in 4 cups of water and secure the lid.
5. Select the 'meat stew' option and cook for 1 hour.
6. 'Natural release' the steam for 30 minutes, and remove the lid.
7. Stuff the calabacita squashes with the pork mixture.
8. Serve hot.

Nutrition Values (Per Serving): Calories: 146| Carbohydrate: 11.5g| Protein: 16.7g| Fat: 4.3g

Instant Pork Thai Curry

Serves: 2

Ingredients

- ½ lbs pork meat, boneless

- ½ cup coconut milk, canned

- 1 tablespoon Thai curry paste

- ¼ cup water

Directions

1. Prepare the Thai curry sauce by mixing the coconut milk, water, and Thai curry paste in a bowl.

2. Put the pork meat and Thai curry sauce into the Air Fryer.

3. Secure the lid and select the 'manual' function. Set to high pressure and cook for 35 minutes.

4. Once done 'Natural release' the steam for 10 minutes, then remove the lid. 5. Serve immediately.

Nutrition Values (Per Serving): Calories: 309 | Carbohydrate: 4.8g | Protein: 25.4g | Fat: 21.3g

Serves: 6

Ingredients

- 2 lbs pork shoulder

- ¾ tablespoon olive oil

- ¼ cup Jamaican jerk spice blend

- ¼ cup beef broth

Directions

1. Use the Jamaican jerk spice with olive oil to marinate the pork for10 minutes.
2. Select the 'sauté' function on the Air Fryer and place the marinated pork inside.
3. Sear each side for 4 minutes, then add the broth.
4. Secure the lid and cook for 45 minutes at high pressure on the manual setting.
5. 'Natural release' the steam for 10 minutes, then remove the lid.
6. Serve hot.

Nutrition Values (Per Serving): Calories: 226| Carbohydrate: 0g (Zero gram)| Protein: 35.4g| Fat: 111.7g

Serves: 4

Ingredients

- 2 lbs baby back pork ribs

- 2 tablespoons apple cider vinegar

- 2 cups apple juice

- 1 tablespoon liquid smoke • ½ teaspoon ground cumin

- ½ teaspoon brown sugar

- ½ teaspoon garlic powder

- ½ teaspoon black pepper

- 1 teaspoon salt

- ¼ cup BBQ sauce

- ¼ cup tomato ketchup
- 1 tablespoon Worcestershire sauce

Directions

1. Combine the salt, pepper, brown sugar, cumin, and garlic powder in a bowl to prepare the seasoning.
2. Add the pork to the mixture and mix well.
3. Now put the seasoned pork, apple cider vinegar, liquid smoke and apple juice into the Air Fryer.
4. Cook for 20 minutes at high pressure using the 'meat stew' function.
5. Once done 'Natural release' the steam for 15 minutes, then remove the lid.
6. Stir in the Worcestershire sauce, BBQ sauce, and tomato ketchup.
7. Let it sit for 15 minutes, then serve hot.

Nutrition Values (Per Serving): Calories: 746 | Carbohydrate: 25.2g | Protein: 36.6g | Fat: 54.5g

Coconut Creamy Chicken

Serves: 4

Ingredients:

- 4 big chicken legs
- 5 tsp. turmeric powder
- 2 tbsp. ginger; grated
- 4 tbsp. coconut cream
- Salt and black pepper to the taste

Directions:

1. In a bowl, mix cream with turmeric, ginger, salt, and pepper, whisk, add chicken pieces, toss them well and leave aside for 2 hours.
2. Transfer chicken to your preheated air fryer, cook at 370 °F, for 25 minutes; divide among plates and serve with a side salad.

Nutrition Facts (Per Serving): Calories: 300; Fat: 4; Fiber: 12; Carbs:22; Protein: 20

Serves: 4

Ingredients:

- 4 duck breasts; boneless, skin on, and scored

- 1 tbsp. ginger; grated

- 1 tsp. cumin; ground

- 1/2 tsp. clove; ground

- 2 cups cherries; pitted

- 1/2 cup sugar

- 1/4 cup honey

- 1/3 cup balsamic vinegar
- 1/2 cup yellow onion; chopped
- 1/2 tsp. cinnamon powder
- 4 sage leaves; chopped
- 1 tsp. garlic; minced
- 1 jalapeno; chopped
- 2 cups rhubarb; sliced
- Salt and black pepper to the taste

Directions:

1. Season duck breast with salt and pepper put in your air fryer and cook at 350 °F, for 5 minutes on each side.
2. Meanwhile; heat a pan over medium heat, add sugar, honey, vinegar, garlic, ginger, cumin, clove, cinnamon, sage, jalapeno, rhubarb, onion, and cherries; stir, bring to a simmer and cook for 10 minutes.
3. Add duck breasts; toss well, divide everything between plates and serve.

Nutrition Facts (Per Serving): Calories: 456; Fat: 13; Fiber: 4; Carbs:64; Protein: 31

Easy Duck Breasts Recipe

Serves: 4

Ingredients:

- 4 duck breasts; skinless and boneless
- 4 garlic heads; peeled, tops cut off and quartered
- 2 tbsp. lemon juice
- 1/2 tsp. lemon pepper
- 1 ½ tbsp. olive oil
- Salt and black pepper to the taste

Directions:

1. In a bowl, mix duck breasts with garlic, lemon juice, salt, pepper, lemon pepper, and olive oil and toss everything.

2. Transfer duck and garlic to your air fryer and cook at 350 °F, for 15 minutes. Divide duck breasts and garlic between plates and serve.

Nutrition Facts (Per Serving): Calories: 200; Fat: 7; Fiber: 1; Carbs: 11; Protein: 17

Duck and Tea Sauce Recipe

Serves: 4

Ingredients:

- 2 duck breast halves; boneless
- 3/4 cup shallot; chopped
- 2 ¼ cup chicken stock
- 1 ½ cup orange juice
- 3 tsp. earl gray tea leaves
- 3 tbsp. butter; melted
- 1 tbsp. honey
- Salt and black pepper to the taste

Directions:

1. Season duck breast halves with salt and pepper put in the preheated air fryer and cook at 360 °F, for 10 minutes.
2. Meanwhile; heat a pan with the butter over medium heat, add shallot; stir and cook for 2-3 minutes. 3. Add stock; stir and cook for another minute.
3. Add orange juice, tea leaves, and honey; stir, cook for 2-3 minutes more and strain into a bowl.
4. Divide duck on plates, drizzle tea sauce all over, and serve.

Nutrition Facts (Per Serving): Calories: 228; Fat: 11; Fiber: 2; Carbs:20; Protein: 12

Chicken and Radish Mix Recipe

Serves: 4

Ingredients:

- 4 chicken things; bone-in

- 1 tbsp. olive oil

- 2 carrots; cut into thin sticks

- 6 radishes; halved

- 2 tbsp. chives; chopped

- 1 cup chicken stock
- 1 tsp. sugar
- Salt and black pepper to the taste

Directions:

1. Heat a pan that fits your air fryer over medium heat, add stock, carrots, sugar, and radishes; stir gently, reduce heat to medium, cover pot partly and simmer for 20 minutes.
2. Rub chicken with olive oil, season with salt and pepper, put in your air fryer, and cook at 350 °F, for 4 minutes. Add chicken to radish mix; toss, introduce everything in your air fryer, cook for 4 minutes more, divide among plates, and serve.

Nutrition Facts (Per Serving): Calories: 237; Fat: 10; Fiber: 4; Carbs:19; Protein: 29

Squid with Teriyaki Sauce

Serves: 4

Ingredients:

- 4 small clean squids
- 2 garlic cloves, chopped
- 4 tbsp. olive oil
- 4 tbsp. Teriyaki sauce
- 1 tbsp. sesame seeds
- Salt and pepper to taste

Directions:

1. Preheat your cooking machine to 140 degrees F.
2. Season the squid with salt and put it into the vacuum bag.
3. Add 2 tbsp. olive oil and chopped garlic
4. Seal the bag, put it into the water bath, and cook for 2 hours.

5. Preheat 2 tbsp. olive oil in the skillet, pour the Teriyaki sauce, and sear the squids on medium to high heat from both sides until brown.

6. Serve sprinkled with sesame seeds.

Nutrition per serving: Calories: 170, Protein: 19 g, Fats: 7 g, Carbs: 8 g

Serves: 4

Ingredients:

- 2 pounds seafood mix, thawed
- 1 cup tomatoes in own juice, diced
- 1/2 cup dry white wine
- 1 bay leaf
- 1 tsp dried oregano
- 2 garlic cloves, minced
- 2 tbsp. olive oil
- Salt and pepper to taste
- Lemon juice for sprinkling

- Chopped parsley for sprinkling

Directions:

1. Preheat your cooking machine to 140 degrees F.
2. Sprinkle the thawed seafood mix with salt and pepper and put it into the vacuum bag adding tomatoes, bay leaf, dried oregano, garlic, olive oil, and white wine.
3. Seal the bag, put it into the water bath, and cook for 2 hours.
4. Serve over rice sprinkled with freshly chopped parsley and lemon juice.

Nutrition per serving: Calories: 370, Protein: 18 g, Fats: 25 g, Carbs: 18 g

Serves: 4

Ingredients:

- 1 pound large shrimp, peeled and deveined

- 1 teaspoon red pepper flakes

- 2 tablespoons olive oil

- 1 teaspoon Tabasco sauce

- 2 tablespoons water

- 1 teaspoon basil, dried

- Salt and black pepper to taste

- 1 tablespoon parsley, chopped

- ½ teaspoon garlic powder

- ½ teaspoon sweet paprika

Directions:

1. In a bowl, mix the shrimp with all other ingredients except the parsley; toss to coat the shrimp well.
2. Place shrimp in the fridge for 2 hours.
3. Transfer the shrimp to your air fryer's basket and cook at 370 degrees F for 10 minutes.
4. Divide into bowls, sprinkle with parsley, and serve with a side salad.

Nutrition: calories 210, fat 7, fiber 6, carbs 13, protein 8

Garlic Potato Wedges in Air Fryer

Serves: 2

Ingredients

- 4 medium potatoes, peeled and cut into wedges
- 4 tablespoons of butter
- 1 teaspoon of chopped cilantro
- 1 cup plain flour
- 1 teaspoon of garlic, minced
- Salt and black pepper, to taste

Directions

1. Soak the potatoes wedges in cold water for about 30 minutes.
2. Then drain and pat dry with a paper towel.
3. Boil water in a large pot and boil the wedges just for 3 minutes.
4. Then take it out on a paper towel.

5. Now in a bowl mix garlic, melted butter, salt, pepper, cilantro and whisk it well.

6. Add the flour to a separate bowl and add salt and black pepper.

7. Then add water to the flour so it gets runny in texture.

8. Now, coat the potatoes with a flour mixture and add it to a foil tin.

9. Put foil tin in the air fryer basket.

10. Now, set time using AIRFRY mode at 390 degrees F for 20 minutes.

11. Once done, serve and enjoy.

Nutritional Information Per Serving: Calories 727 | Fat 24.1g | Sodium. 191mg | Carbs 115.1g | Fiber 12g | Sugar 5.1g | Protein14 g

Serves: 4

Ingredients

- 1 cup cauliflower florets
- 1 cup of carrots, peeled chopped
- 1 cup broccoli florets
- 2 tablespoons of avocado oil
- Salt, to taste
- ½ teaspoon of chili powder
- ½ teaspoon of garlic powder
- ½ teaspoon of herbs de Provence
- 1 cup parmesan cheese

Directions

1. Take a bowl, and add all the veggies to it.

2. Toss and then season the veggies with salt, chili powder, garlic powder, and herbs de Provence.

3. Toss it all well and then drizzle avocado oil.

4. Make sure the ingredients are coated well.

5. Now transfer the veggies to the basket of the air fryer.

6. Turn on the start button and set it to AIR FRY mode at 390 degrees for 10-12 minutes.

7. After 8 minutes of cooking, select the pause button and then take out the basket and sprinkle Parmesan cheese on top of the veggies.

8. Then let the cooking cycle complete for the next 3-4 minutes.

Nutritional Information Per Serving: Calories161 | Fat 9.3g| Sodium434 mg | Carbs 7.7g | Fiber 2.4g | Sugar 2.5g | Protein 13.9

Serves: 2

Ingredients

- 2 pounds Brussels sprouts

- 2 tablespoons avocado oil

- Salt and pepper, to taste

- 1 cup pine nuts, roasted

Directions

1. Trim the bottom of Brussels sprouts.

2. Take a bowl and combine the avocado oil, salt, and black pepper.

3. Toss the Brussels sprouts well.

4. Transfer it to the air fryer basket.

5. Use AIR fry mode for 20 minutes at 390 degrees F.

6. Once the Brussels sprouts get crisp and tender, take out and serve.

Variation Tip: Use olive oil instead of avocado oil

Nutritional Information Per Serving: Calories 672| Fat 50g| Sodium 115mg | Carbs 51g | Fiber 20.2g | Sugar 12.3g|Protein25g

Serves: 4

Ingredients

- 2 red peppers, thinly sliced into strips

- 2 yellow peppers, thinly sliced

- 1 green pepper, thinly sliced

- 2 cups tomato puree

- 1 red onion, thinly sliced into strips

- 2 garlic cloves

- 1 bunch parsley, chopped

- 1 tablespoon olive oil

- Salt and black pepper to taste

Directions

1. Add the oil and all the vegetables to the Air Fryer.

2. Select "Sauté" and stir-fry for 5 minutes with constant stirring.

3. Stir in tomato puree, salt, and pepper.

4. Secure the lid and select the "Manual" function for 5 minutes at high pressure.

5. After the beep, do a quick release and remove the lid.

6. Stir well and serve.

Nutrition Values (Per Serving): Calories: 132, Carbohydrate: 23.7g, Protein: 4.1g, Fat: 4.2g

Serves: 4:

Ingredients:

- 8 ounces tempeh, cut into 12 equal cubes

- 2 cups warm water

- 2 teaspoons sea salt

- 1/2 teaspoon ground turmeric

- 1 teaspoon canola oil or avocado oil

- 2 teaspoons Tofino Fish Sauce or 1 teaspoon low-sodium soy sauce

- mixed with 1/4 teaspoon dulse flakes
- 4 cloves garlic
- 1/2 cup finely chopped onion
- 1 teaspoon chili garlic paste
- 1 teaspoon tamarind paste
- 2 tablespoons tomato paste
- 2 tablespoons water
- 2 teaspoons ponzu sauce

Directions:

1. Place the tempeh in a medium bowl. In a medium measuring cup, mix the warm water and salt and pour over the tempeh. Let the tempeh soak for 5 to 10 minutes.

2. Drain the tempeh and return it to the bowl. Add the turmeric, oil, and Tofino Fish Sauce, tossing with tongs to coat well.

3. Transfer the tempeh cubes to the air fryer basket. Cook at 320°F for 10 minutes. Shake the air fryer basket, increase the heat to 400°F, and cook for 5 minutes longer.

4. While the tempeh is in the air fryer, combine the garlic, onion, chili garlic paste, tamarind paste, tomato paste, water, and ponzu sauce in a food processor and pulse for 20 to 30 seconds. Transfer this mixture to a medium saucepan and bring it to a rapid boil on medium-high heat. Cover the sauce, reduce the heat to low, and simmer for 10 minutes.

5. Transfer the cooked tempeh to the saucepan and toss it in the sauce with a spoon or tongs to coat each piece well. Cover and simmer on low for 5 minutes.

Serve 4:

Ingredients:

- 8 ounces tempeh
- 3/4 cup low-sodium vegetable broth
- Juice of 2 lemons
- 1/4 cup low-sodium tamari or soy sauce
- 2 teaspoons extra-virgin olive oil
- 1 teaspoon maple syrup or dark agave syrup
- 2 teaspoons ground cumin

- 1 teaspoon ground turmeric
- 1/2 teaspoon ground black pepper
- 3 cloves garlic, minced
- 1 medium red onion, quartered
- 1 small green bell pepper, thinly sliced
- 1 cup sliced, stemmed button mushrooms
- 1 cup halved cherry tomatoes

Directions:

1. Steam the tempeh for 10 minutes in a saucepan on the stove. Alternatively, steam the tempeh for 1 minute on low pressure in an Air Fryer or pressure cooker; use a quick release. Combine the broth, lemon juice, tamari, oil, maple syrup, cumin, turmeric, pepper, and garlic in a medium bowl. Set aside.

2. Cut the tempeh into 12 cubes. Transfer them to an airtight container. Place the vegetables in a second airtight container. Pour half of the marinade over the tempeh and half over the vegetables. Cover both and refrigerate for 2 hours (or up to overnight). Drain the tempeh and vegetables, reserving the marinade.

3. Thread 4 cubes of tempeh, alternating each with the vegetables, on a skewer to make a kabob. Repeat this process to make 3 more kabobs. Place the kabobs in the air fryer basket or on the rack accessory. (If you are using a smaller air fryer, you may have to cook in two batches.) Cook at 390°F for 5 minutes. Turn the kabobs and drizzle the remaining marinade over them. Cook for 5 more minutes.

Baked Gigante Beans

Serve 2:

Ingredients:

- 1 1/2 cups cooked or canned butter beans or great Northern beans, rinsed and drained

- 1 teaspoon extra-virgin olive oil or canola oil

- 1 small onion, cut into 1/8-inch thick half-moon slices

- 1 clove garlic, minced

- 1 (8-ounce) can tomato sauce

- 1 tablespoon coarsely chopped fresh parsley

- 1/2 teaspoon dried oregano

- 1/2 teaspoon vegan chicken bouillon granules or salt (optional)

- 1/4 teaspoon freshly ground black pepper

Directions:

1. Place the beans in an air fryer–safe casserole dish or pan.

2. Heat the oil in a medium saucepan on medium-high heat. Add the onion and garlic and sauté for 5 minutes. Add the tomato sauce,

parsley, oregano, and bouillon granules. Bring the mixture to a boil, cover the saucepan, reduce the heat to low, and simmer for 3 minutes.

3. Preheat the air fryer to 360°F for 3 minutes. Pour the tomato mixture over the beans and mix well. Sprinkle the pepper over the beans. Place the beans in the air fryer basket. Cook at 360°F for 8 minutes.

Serve 1:

Ingredients:

- ≥ ounces prepared Pizza Dough (see here) or store-bought vegan pizza dough

- 2 spritzes extra-virgin olive oil

- 1/3 cup pizza sauce

- 1/3 cup non-dairy shredded mozzarella cheese, divided

- 1/2 onion, cut into 1/8-inch thick half-moon slices

- 1/4 cup sliced mushrooms

- 2 to 3 black or green olives, pitted and sliced

- 4 fresh basil leaves

Directions:

1. Place the pizza dough on a lightly floured work surface and roll it cut or use your hands to press it out (keeping in mind the size of your air fryer basket, to assure it fits). Spritz the dough with the oil

and place the dough, oiled side down, into the air fryer basket. Cook at 390°F for 4 to 5 minutes.

2. Once the dough is precooked, open the air fryer—use caution, as the basket is hot—and spread the sauce over the dough. Sprinkle half the cheese over the sauce. Add the onion, mushrooms, olives, and basil. Sprinkle the remaining cheese over the toppings.

3. Cook at 390°F for 6 minutes (or 7 to 8 minutes for a very crisp crust). Use a spatula to remove the pizza from the air fryer.

Serve 4:

Ingredients:

- 4 vegan hot dogs

- 2 teaspoons non-dairy butter

- 4 Pretzel Hot Dog Buns or store-bought vegan hot dog buns

Directions:

1. Slice the hot dogs lengthwise without cutting through them. Spread the hot dogs out flat, cut-side up. Spread 1/2 teaspoon butter on each hot dog.

2. Place the hot dogs, buttered side down, in the air fryer. Cook at 390°F for 3 minutes. Remove and set aside.

3. Place the hot dog buns in the air fryer and heat at 400°F for 1 minute to lightly toast them. Serve the hot dogs in the buns with your favorite condiments.

Serves: 1

Ingredients:

- 1 teaspoon salt
- ½ teaspoon black pepper
- ½ teaspoon ground cumin
- ¼ teaspoon cayenne
- 1 (1- to 1½-pound) whole red snapper, cleaned and patted dry
- 2 tablespoons olive oil
- 2 garlic cloves, minced
- ¼ cup fresh dill
- Lemon wedges, for serving

Directions:

1. . Preheat the air fryer to 360°F

2. . In a small bowl, mix the salt, pepper, cumin, and cayenne.

3. . Coat the outside of the fish with olive oil, then sprinkle the seasoning blend over the outside of the fish. Stuff the minced garlic and dill inside the cavity of the fish.

4. . Place the snapper into the basket of the air fryer and roast for 20 minutes. Flip the snapper over, and roast for 15 minutes more, or until the snapper reaches an internal temperature of 145°F.

PER SERVING: Calories: 125; Total Fat: 2g; Saturated Fat: 0g; Protein: 23g; Total Carbohydrates: 2g; Fiber: 0g; Sugar: 0g; Cholesterol: 42mg

Seasoned Tuna Steaks

Serves: 4

Ingredients:

- 1 teaspoon garlic powder

- ½ teaspoon salt

- ¼ teaspoon dried thyme

- ¼ teaspoon dried oregano

- 4 tuna steaks

- 2 tablespoons olive oil

- 1 lemon, quartered

Directions:

1. . Preheat the air fryer to 380°F.

2. . In a small bowl, whisk together the garlic powder, salt, thyme, and oregano.

3. . Coat the tuna steaks with olive oil. Season both sides of each steak with the seasoning blend. Place the steaks in a single layer in the air fryer basket.
4. . Cook for 5 minutes, then flip and cook for an additional 3 to 4 minutes.

PER SERVING: Calories: 269; Total Fat: 14g; Saturated Fat: 3g; Protein: 33g; Total Carbohydrates: 1g; Fiber: 0g; Sugar: 0g; Cholesterol: 54mg

Serves: 4

Ingredients:

- ¼ cup raw honey

- 4 garlic cloves, minced

- 1 tablespoon olive oil

- ½ teaspoon salt

- Olive oil cooking spray

- 4 (1½-inch-thick) salmon fillets

Directions:

1. . Preheat the air fryer to 380°F.

2. . In a small bowl, mix the honey, garlic, olive oil, and salt.

3. . Spray the bottom of the air fryer basket with olive oil cooking spray, and place the salmon in a single layer on the bottom of the air fryer basket.

4. . Brush the top of each fillet with the honey-garlic mixture, and roast for 10 to 12 minutes, or until the internal temperature reaches 145°F.

PER SERVING: Calories: 260; Total Fat: 11g; Saturated Fat: 2g; Protein: 23g; Total Carbohydrates: 18g; Fiber: 0g; Sugar: 17g; Cholesterol: 62mg

Balsamic-Garlic Shrimp

Serves: 2

Ingredients:

- ½ cup olive oil
- 4 garlic cloves, minced
- 1 tablespoon balsamic vinegar
- ¼ teaspoon cayenne pepper
- ¼ teaspoon salt
- 1 Roma tomato, diced

- ¼ cup Kalamata olives
- 1 pound medium shrimp, cleaned and deveined

Directions:

1. Preheat the air fryer to 380°F.
2. In a small bowl, combine the olive oil, garlic, balsamic, cayenne, and salt.
3. . Divide the tomatoes and olives among four small ramekins. Then divide shrimp among the ramekins, and pour a quarter of the oil mixture over the shrimp.
4. . Cook for 6 to 8 minutes, or until the shrimp are cooked through.

PER SERVING: Calories: 160; Total Fat: 9g; Saturated Fat: 1g; Protein: 16g; Total Carbohydrates: 4g; Fiber: 1g; Sugar: 1g; Cholesterol: 143mg

Salmon Burgers with Creamy Broccoli Slaw

Serves: 2

Ingredients:

For the salmon burgers

- 1 pound salmon fillets, bones, and skin removed
- 1 egg
- ¼ cup fresh dill, chopped
- 1 cup whole wheat bread crumbs
- 1 teaspoon salt
- ½ teaspoon cayenne pepper
- 2 garlic cloves, minced

- 4 whole-wheat buns

  For the broccoli slaw

- 3 cups chopped or shredded broccoli

- ½ cup shredded carrots

- ¼ cup sunflower seeds

- 2 garlic cloves, minced

- ½ teaspoon salt

- 2 tablespoons apple cider vinegar

- 1 cup nonfat plain Greek yogurt

Directions:

To make the salmon burgers

1. . Preheat the air fryer to 360°F.
2. . In a food processor, pulse the salmon fillets until they are finely chopped.
3. . In a large bowl, combine the chopped salmon, egg, dill, bread crumbs, salt, cayenne, and garlic until it comes together.
4. . Form the salmon into 4 patties. Place them into the air fryer basket, making sure that they don't touch each other.
5. . Bake for 5 minutes. Flip the salmon patties and bake for 5 minutes more.

To make the broccoli slaw

6. . In a large bowl, combine all of the ingredients for the broccoli slaw. Mix well.
7. . Serve the salmon burgers on toasted whole wheat buns, and top with a generous portion of broccoli slaw.

PER SERVING: Calories: 523; Total Fat: 16g; Saturated Fat: 3g; Protein: 41g; Total Carbohydrates: 51g; Fiber: 5g; Sugar: 8g; Cholesterol: 112mg

Parsnip Fries with Garlic-Yogurt Dip

Serves: 4

Ingredients:

- 3 medium parsnips, peeled, cut into sticks
- ¼ teaspoon kosher salt
- 1 teaspoon olive oil
- 1 garlic clove, unpeeled
- Cooking spray

  Dip:

- ¼ cup plain Greek yogurt
- ⅛ teaspoon garlic powder
- 1 tablespoon sour cream
- ¼ teaspoon kosher salt
- Freshly ground black pepper, to taste

Directions:

1. Spritz the air fryer basket with cooking spray.
2. Put the parsnip sticks in a large bowl, then sprinkle with salt and drizzle with olive oil.
3. Transfer the parsnip into the basket and add the garlic.
4. Put the air fryer basket on the baking pan and slide into Rack Position 2, select Air Fry, set temperature to 360°F (182°C), and set time to 10 minutes.
5. Stir the parsnip halfway through the cooking time.
6. Meanwhile, peel the garlic and crush it. Combine the crushed garlic with the ingredients for the dip. Stir to mix well.
7. When cooked, the parsnip sticks should be crisp. Remove the parsnip fries from the oven and serve with the dipping sauce.

Simple Air Fried Okra Chips

Serves: 6

Ingredients:

- 2 pounds (907 g) fresh okra pods, cut into 1-inch pieces
- 2 tablespoons canola oil
- 1 teaspoon coarse sea salt

Directions:

8. Stir the oil and salt in a bowl to mix well. Add the okra and toss to coat well. Place the okra in the air fryer basket.

9. Put the air fryer basket on the baking pan and slide into Rack Position 2, select Air Fry, set temperature to 400°F (205°C), and set time to 16 minutes.

10. Flip the okra at least three times during cooking.

11. When cooked, the okra should be lightly browned. Remove from the oven and serve immediately.

Serves: 9

Ingredients:

- 3 cups shelled raw peanuts
- 1 tablespoon hot red pepper sauce
- 3 tablespoons granulated white sugar

Directions:

1. Put the peanuts in a large bowl, then drizzle with hot red pepper sauce and sprinkle with sugar. Toss to coat well.

2. Pour the peanuts in the air fryer basket.

3. Put the air fryer basket on the baking pan and slide into Rack Position 2, select Air Fry, set temperature to 400°F (205°C), and set time to 5 minutes.

4. Stir the peanuts halfway through the cooking time.

5. When cooking is complete, the peanuts will be crispy and browned. Remove from the oven and serve immediately.

Lemony and Garlicky Asparagus

Serves: 10 spears

Ingredients:

- 10 spears asparagus (about ½ pound / 227 g in total), snap the ends off
- 1 tablespoon lemon juice
- 2 teaspoons minced garlic
- ½ teaspoon salt
- ¼ teaspoon ground black pepper
- Cooking spray

Directions:

1. Line the air fryer basket with parchment paper.

2. Put the asparagus spears in a large bowl. Drizzle with lemon juice and sprinkle with minced garlic, salt, and ground black pepper. Toss to coat well.

3. Transfer the asparagus to the basket and spritz with cooking spray.

4. Put the air fryer basket on the baking pan and slide into Rack Position 2, select Air Fry, set temperature to 400°F (205°C), and set time to 10 minutes.

5. Flip the asparagus halfway through cooking.

6. When cooked, the asparagus should be wilted and soft. Remove from the oven and serve immediately.

Spanakopita

Serves: 6

Ingredients:

- ½ (10-ounce / 284-g) package frozen spinach, thawed and squeezed dry
- 1 egg, lightly beaten
- ¼ cup pine nuts, toasted
- ¼ cup grated Parmesan cheese
- ¾ cup crumbled feta cheese
- ⅛ teaspoon ground nutmeg
- ½ teaspoon salt
- Freshly ground black pepper, to taste
- 6 sheets phyllo dough
- ½ cup butter, melted

Directions:

1. Combine all the ingredients, except for the phyllo dough and butter, in a large bowl. Whisk to combine well. Set aside.

2. Place a sheet of phyllo dough on a clean work surface. Brush with butter then top with another layer sheet of phyllo. Brush with butter then cut the layered sheets into six 3-inch-wide strips.

3. Top each strip with 1 tablespoon of the spinach mixture, then fold the bottom left corner over the mixture towards the right strip edge to make a triangle. Keep folding triangles until each strip is folded over.

4. Brush the triangles with butter and repeat with remaining strips and phyllo dough.

5. Place the triangles in the baking pan.

6. Put the air fryer basket on the baking pan and slide into Rack Position 2, select Air Fry, set temperature to 350°F (180°C), and set time to 8 minutes.

7. Flip the triangles halfway through the cooking time.

8. When cooking is complete, the triangles should be golden brown. Remove from the oven and serve immediately.

Serves: 2

Ingredients:

- 2 garlic cloves, minced
- 1 tsp cayenne pepper
- 2 tsp mustard powder
- tbsp olive oil
- 2 tbsp freshly ground black pepper
- 1 tsp salt
- 1 tsp onion powder

Directions:

1. Whisk all the ingredients in a small bowl.
2. Rub the mixture into the beef or pork and cook according to the Directions.

3. This rub is ideal for cooking pork and beef.

4. You can scale the number of ingredients depending on the amount of meat you are going to cook Air Fryer.

Nutrition per serving: Calories: 120, Protein: 0 g, Fats: 14 g, Carbs: 0 g

Serves: 2

Ingredients:

- 2 garlic cloves, minced
- 1/3 cup ground paprika
- 1 tsp freshly ground black pepper
- 1 tsp chili powder
- 1 tsp onion powder
- 1 tsp salt

Directions:

1. Mix all the ingredients in a small bowl.
2. Rub the mixture into the beef or pork and cook according to the Directions.
3. This rub is ideal for cooking pork and beef.

4. You can scale the number of ingredients depending on the amount of meat you are going to cook Air Fryer.

Nutrition per serving: Calories: 8, Protein: 0 g, Fats: 0 g, Carbs: 1 g

Serves: 4

Ingredients

- 2 tuber fennel
- 1 g saffron
- 100 ml poultry stock
- 20 ml olive oil
- 3 g salt

Directions

1. Cut the fennel lengthways into approximately 6 mm thick slices. Where the leaves hang together through the stalk, the slices result.

2. The stems and the outer parts can be used well for a fennel cream soup.

3. Vacuum the slices together with the other ingredients in a vacuum bag. Cook in a water bath at 85 ° C for 3 hours.

4. Remove from the bags and reduce the cooking stock to approx. 1/3 of the amount.

5. A wonderful and effective side dish, for example with meat and fish dishes.

Roast beef with walnut crust

Serves: 4

Ingredients

- 1 kg roast beef
- 150 g Walnuts, chopped
- 1½ tbsp. butter
- 50 g Parmesan, finely sliced
- 4 tbsp. Herbs, chopped, Mediterranean
- Salt and pepper

Directions

1. Season the roast beef with salt and pepper first. Then weld in a vacuum. Cook the roast beef at 63 ° C using the Air Fryer Directions for about 4 - 5 hours.

2. In the meantime, create a crust from the walnuts, butter, parmesan, herbs, salt, and pepper. It is best to put all the mixed ingredients in a freezer bag. In this, you roll the ingredients flat to the required size. Then the crust goes in the fridge. Later you can cut the crust to the right size with a sharp knife including foil. Remove the foil and distribute it exactly on the meat.

3. Preheat the oven to 220 ° C grill function 20 minutes before serving and at the end of the cooking time.

4. Fry the roast beef in a very hot pan with little fat on each side for a very short time (30 seconds).

5. Remove the roast beef from the pan and place it in a baking dish. Now put the crust on the meat. Put in the oven and take out the meat only when the crust is nice and brown. However, this does not take long, at most 5 minutes.

6. Now you can enjoy a perfect pink roast beef with a crust. B. with leek vegetables and spaetzle.

Serves: 2

Ingredients

- 400 g Beef fillet (centerpiece)

- 1 tbsp. Worcester sauce

- ½ tsp Pimentón de la Vera, mild

- 1 teaspoon Paprika powder, spicy

- 1 tsp, heaped raw cane sugar

- 1 tsp, heaped Chives, dr.

Directions

1. Total time approx. 15 hours 10 minutes

2. Place the fillet in a vacuum bag. Mix all other ingredients and add to the bag. Rub the fillet with the ingredients in the bag. Then vacuum. It is best to let the fillet marinate overnight.

3. Remove the fillet from the refrigerator 2 hours before cooking. Preheat a Air Fryer suitable oven to 55 ° C. Place the fillet in the oven for 3 hours.

4. Take out of the bag, cut open and serve immediately.

Index

B

C

D

E

F

G

S

T

Cooking Conversion Chart

TEMPERATURE		WEIGHT	
FAHRENHEIT	**CELSIUS**	**IMPERIAL**	**METRIC**
100 °F	37 °C	1/2 oz	15 g
150 °F	65 °C	1 oz	29 g
200 °F	93 °C	2 oz	57 g
250 °F	121 °C	3 oz	85 g
300 °F	150 °C	4 oz	113 g
325 °F	160 °C	5 oz	141 g
350 °F	180 °C	6 oz	170 g
375 °F	190 °C	8 oz	227 g
400 °F	200 °C	10 oz	283 g
425 °F	220 °C	12 oz	340 g
450 °F	230 °C	13 oz	369 g
500 °F	260 °C	14 oz	397 g
525 °F	270 °C	15 oz	425 g
550 °F	288 °C	1 lb	453 g

MEASUREMENT			
CUP	**ONCES**	**MILLILITERS**	**TABLESPOON**
1/16 cup	1/2 oz	15 ml	1
1/8 cup	1 oz	30 ml	3
1/4 cup	2 oz	59 ml	4
1/3 cup	2.5 oz	79 ml	5.5
3/8 cup	3 oz	90 ml	6
1/2 cup	4 oz	118 ml	8
2/3 cup	5 oz	158 ml	11
3/4 cup	6 oz	177 ml	12
1 cup	8 oz	240 ml	16
2 cup	16 oz	480 ml	32
4 cup	32 oz	960 ml	64
5 cup	40 oz	1180 ml	80
6 cup	48 oz	1420 ml	96
8 cup	64 oz	1895 ml	128

CPSIA information can be obtained
at www.ICGtesting.com
Printed in the USA
BVHW091929230621
610293BV00008B/1146